THE CULTURE TRAP

helping teens deal with the world around them

Dave McCasland

VICTOR BOOKS

a division of SP Publications, Inc.
WHEATON, ILLINOIS 60187

Offices also in Fullerton, California • Whitby, Ontario, Canada • Amersham-on-the-Hill, Bucks, England

Bible quotations are from the <u>New International Version</u>,
© 1978 by the New York International Bible Society.

Library of Congress Catalog Card Number: 82-61007

ISBN: 0-88207-191-2

CONTENTS

INTRODUCTION   4

1   IDENTITY: THE BASIC ISSUE 6

2   COMMITMENT: THE THINGS WE SAY YES TO IN LIFE 12

3   EXPECTATIONS: CATCH-22 FOR EVERYONE 16

4   RIGHTS: SOCIETY'S NEW BATTLEGROUND 21

5   EDUCATION: THE ONE SIZE THAT DOESN'T FIT ALL 25

6   DIVORCE AND THE CHANGING FAMILY 29

7   PEER PRESSURE: WHERE THE RUBBER MEETS THE ROAD 35

8   MASS MEDIA MAZE: LOOKING, LISTENING, LEARNING 39

9   LOVE IN THE AFTERNOON: WANDERING IN A SEXUAL WILDERNESS 44

10   ARTIFICIAL ADULTHOOD: THE TRAPPINGS OF INDEPENDENCE 49

11   SERVICE: WHAT WE ALL WANT TO GET AND FEW WANT TO GIVE 54

12   RESCUE THE PERISHING: OR LET THEM LEARN TO SWIM 58

CONCLUSION 64

INTRODUCTION

Imagine that you have taken a group of teenagers sailing on a large lake. Suddenly, a storm sweeps across the lake, capsizing your boat and hurling all of you into the water. You are still responsible for the safety of those teens but now you have an additional problem--your own survival. You need to help those kids, but at the same time you are facing the same circumstances they face.

That's what it's like for any adult--youth worker, parent, or friend --when it comes to helping teens cope with culture. We are immersed in the same waters of society through which they must struggle. We do not have the luxury of standing on the shore and tossing spiritual life preservers out to adolescents. In addition to our tasks of supervision and support, we must also swim.

In this book, we will look at several critical areas in which today's teens must cope with culture. It will come as no surprise to find that we haven't arrived, but are still struggling with these things our-selves. How well we are coping determines whether we are part of the problem or part of the solution for the teens in our lives.

May God enable us to provide the leadership and encouragement so desperately wanted and needed by teens in our society today.

Sincerely,

Dave McCasland

Dave McCasland

As the author, I would rate the value of this book to you according to the following scale:

Reading the book through once, chuckling occasionally, and every so often thinking, "That's interesting. I should try that."

Actually discussing the questions at the end of each chapter in your youth group or family.

Writing the answers to the questions directed to you as a youth director or parent.

Taking action in your personal life so that you begin to cope with culture more effectively as an adult Christian.

This book is directed at youth workers and parents because we share the job of training teenagers in Christian faith and living. We need each other and we need to work together.

1 IDENTITY: THE BASIC ISSUE

> "I am afraid to tell you who I am, because if I tell you who I am, you may not like who I am, and that's all I have."
> --John Powell

> "It is high time that we declare all-out war on the destructive value system . . . which reserves self-worth and dignity for a select minority. <u>Every</u> child is entitled to hold up his head, not in haughtiness and pride, but in confidence and security." --Dr. James Dobson

Ask any youth worker, teacher, psychologist, or parent to name the most critical things with which teenagers must cope and toward the top of every list will be <u>IDENTITY</u>. Why is this business of self-image so tough for teens?

For one thing, adolescence is a time of transition and change. A teen's self-concept has been molded primarily by his family up to this point. Now it is being defined more by friends. It's important for us as adults to:
1. Realize that this is happening.
2. Help our teens understand <u>how</u> this is happening.
3. Assure them that it's OK <u>for</u> it to happen. It's a natural and necessary part of their growing into independent persons.

    Another reason that identity is difficult for teens is the number
of conflicting and confusing ways for deciding who we are. For
example:

CULTURALLY DEFINED Most of society operates on the premise that
you're a neat person if you are any one or a combination of the
following: pretty, handsome, athletic, intelligent, wealthy,
sexually aware and/or active, well-dressed, popular. If you don't
fit into at least one of these categories, your value is low.

PARENTALLY DEFINED Dr. James Oraker, staff psychologist for Young
Life says, "For better or worse, the parent is the most important
person in the life of a teen." Some parents convince their children
that they are of great worth to them, to others, and to God. Other
parents communicate just the opposite. What parents think, say, and
do is still vitally important to teens.

DIVINELY DEFINED God has made it clear in the Bible and in the Person
of Jesus Christ, that each person is priceless to Him. If a teen
personally accepts this critical truth, it will make a significant
difference in his or her attitude toward all of life. Yet, it's helpful to remember that few of us ever get this message just by reading.
We come to believe it when others treat us with the same value God
places on us.

PERSONALLY DEFINED Eventually, each teen must sift through all the
definitions of who he is and what he is worth and come up with a
personal conviction on the matter. A healthy, biblically based
identity will provide a solid foundation for building a life. Anything less than that is a step in the direction of eventual
disappointment.

THE McCASLAND "ADOLESCENT ICEBERG"
(A PERSONAL THEORY)

In order to visualize the importance of identity in a teen's life, consider the following illustration.

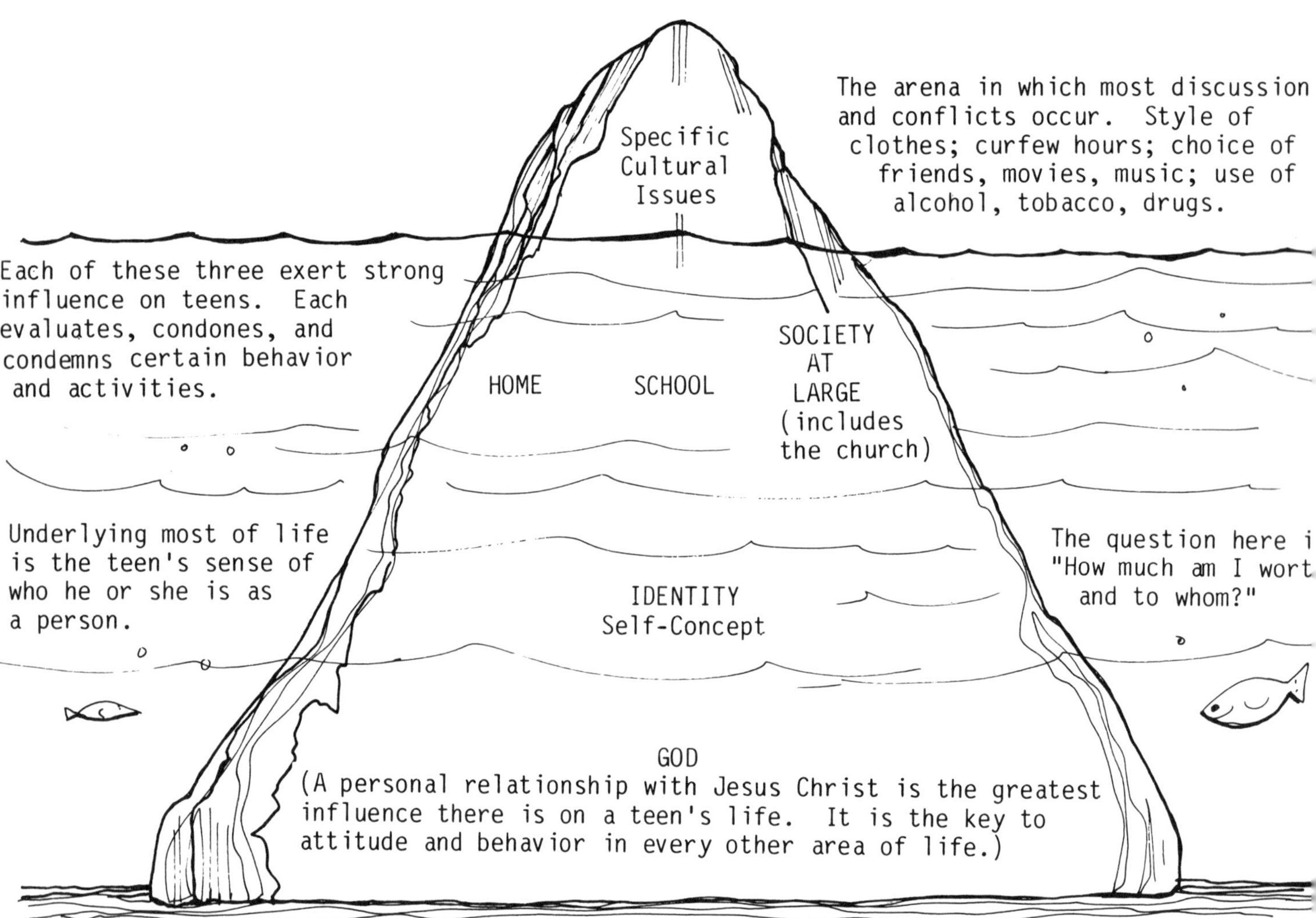

In our efforts to help teens cope with culture, we have to deal with more than the tip of the iceberg. We must get past the specific cultural issues that occupy prominence above the surface, and help teens develop their concepts of who they are as persons.

DISCUSSION WITH OLDER TEENS

(1) Who are you?
Ask your high schoolers to answer this question by writing five
different things they are. They should not use their names or
their relationships to anyone. Some possible answers could be:
I am: a Christian; a friend; a student; a musician.

After they list their first five answers and you discuss them,
try for another five.

(2) Ask your teens how they think each of the following has shaped
their ideas of who they are:

Parents--

Friends--

School--

Television and Films--

Advertising--

Church--

(3) How do the following Bible passages affect your self-concept?

Genesis 1:26-28

Psalm 139:1-6

Psalm 139:13-18

Matthew 10:29-31

1 John 4:9-10

(4) What do you think is the key to overcoming a sense of inferiority?

(5) What can I do to help those around me to feel better about
themselves?

DISCUSSION WITH YOUNGER TEENS

(1) How do you feel about yourself when you run for a school office and get elected?

(2) How do you feel about yourself when you try out for something (athletic teams, cheerleading, school play) and don't make it?

(3) When you fail at one thing, what helps you avoid feeling like a failure at everything?

(4) If you could trade places with anyone in the world, who would it be and why?

(5) If you could change one thing about yourself, what would you change and why? (Be sensitive to your group's willingness to discuss this question. It might be better for them to think about it quietly for a few minutes without answering aloud.)

LOOK IN THE MIRROR
FOR YOUTH WORKERS AND PARENTS

(1) How would it affect your self-concept if you:

a. Lost your job?

b. Became divorced?

c. Were facially disfigured in an accident?

d. Had a child who turned against God?

(2) What everyday events in the life of your teens (at church or at home) do you think are most important in shaping their self-concepts?

(3) In what ways can you best help the teens in your life to develop healthy, biblical concepts of themselves?

SUMMARY

A question asked every day by every teen is "How important am I and to whom?" Learning who we are, what we are, and how important we are is very much a part of the cultural water in which we all swim.
    For the most part, we learn how important we are by the way others treat us. We should help teens explore and determine their identities, but we must also treat them with dignity and respect, with the same importance God has placed on each of them.

RECOMMENDED READING

Hide or Seek by Dr. James Dobson. Fleming H. Revell Co. One of the finest books available on strategies for developing self-esteem in children and teens.

Why Am I Afraid To Tell You Who I Am? by John Powell. Argus. Helpful insights into self-awareness, growth, and communication.

2 COMMITMENT: THE THINGS WE SAY YES TO IN LIFE

"When Jesus tells you to take up your cross daily, He is not telling you to find some way to suffer daily. He is simply giving fair warning of what happens to the person who follows Him." --John White

Often our approach to helping teens deal with culture involves an effort to insure their ability to say no to the temptations of youth. We are understandably concerned that they avoid as many pitfalls as possible during their adolescent years.

But as I have researched this Power Pak, I have become more aware than ever of our need to help teens say YES to the most important things and the most important Person in life. When a teen says yes to Jesus Christ in a commitment to personal faith and discipleship, he or she has taken a quantum leap forward in life. If it is true that "If anyone is in Christ, he is a new creation; the old has gone, the new has come!" (2 Cor. 5:17, NIV) then helping teens make that important commitment to Jesus Christ is the greatest thing we can do in helping them cope with culture.

As a Christian, a teen has the presence of the changeless Christ to guide him through a changing culture. In the midst of a program-oriented society and, yes, even a program-oriented church, we need to guide our teens toward those life-changing personal yes decisions.

Everyone is committed to something.

In the 1960s, it seemed that the youth of our nation were committed to the establishment of a new social and political order through the overthrow of the existing one.

In the '70s, observers spoke of the self-absorption of the "Me Decade." Many people were committed to nothing more than satisfying themselves. But commitment, like anything else in culture, changes.

Today, we seem to be back on the track of a modified success ethic strangely reminiscent of the 1950s.

> A recent poll conducted by UCLA and the
>
> American Council on Education found that
>
> 63% of college freshmen rated "being well
>
> off financially" a top goal.

Social scientist Daniel Yankelovich has said: "There is something about our times that stimulates Americans to take big risks in pursuit of new conceptions of the good life. Perhaps more than anything else, this freedom to make one's own choices in living . . . distinguishes us from our parents' generation." (Parade Magazine May 24, 1981)

It's difficult to predict what most people in society will be committed to in the next 5 to 10 years, but whatever it is, teens will be influenced by it.

What we must do is help teens determine what society is saying about commitment and how it compares with God's call to each of us in Jesus Christ.

DISCUSSION WITH OLDER TEENS

(1) Write the following statement on a chalkboard, or put it on an overhead projector:

"We students have been condemned . . . as the 'uncommitted generation.' We admit the truth of the designation, but protest the implication we are uncommitted whether through choice or indifference. To the contrary, most of us are deeply concerned over our lack of commitment and many of us are actually searching for that cause to which we can offer unreserved allegiance. If we do belong to the 'uncommitted generation' it is because the church has not called us to her Lord or her mission clearly enough to excite our response."

(2) Discuss together:

a. Who do you think said this? When? Where? Why?

b. Do you feel the same or differently? Why?

(The statement was made in 1958 by some 3,400 college students gathered in Lawrence, Kansas for the sixth quadrennial Methodist Student Conference.)

(3) What are the two most important commitments society says you should make?

(4) What do you think are the two most important commitments God wants you to make? (Point your high schoolers to Matt. 22:34-39.)

(5) What do you think it means to be committed to Jesus Christ?

(6) How does your commitment to Christ affect your decisions?

(7) How do you decide whether a commitment you have made can be broken or whether you must keep it at all costs?

DISCUSSION WITH YOUNGER TEENS

(1) Can you think of a time when someone made a commitment to you and then broke it?   How did it make you feel?

(2) Is there anything on which you would give your word and never back down?   If so, what is it, and why?

(3) Are there any commitments you have made to God?   If so, how do they affect the way you live every day?

(4) What is your opinion of a person who says one thing and usually does another?

LOOK IN THE MIRROR
FOR YOUTH WORKERS AND PARENTS

(1) List five things that you feel society today is saying to teens about commitment.

(2) List five things that you believe <u>God</u> is saying to teens about commitment.

(3) List the five most important commitments in your own life and write one thing you are doing to keep each of them.

(4) Take a poll among parents of your youth. Try sending home a question on a 3" x 5" card, with a self-addressed stamped envelope to get it back to you. Possible questions:

"If the church could help you teach your teenager one thing about commitment, what would it be?"

"I would like to see my teenager become more committed to . . ." (Please complete this statement.)

"The most important thing I think my teenager doesn't yet understand about commitment is . . ." (Please complete.)

SUMMARY

Instead of focusing exclusively on teaching our teens to say no, let's pour maximum effort into helping them be prepared to say <u>yes</u> to Jesus Christ and to His way. Teens need to understand how society defines and values commitment, and how that view affects them.

RECOMMENDED READING

<u>The Cost of Commitment</u> by John White. InterVarsity Press. A small book with keen insight on what it means to be a 20th-century follower of Jesus Christ.

<u>How to Disciple Your Children</u> by Walter A. Henrichsen. Victor Books. Practical advice for helping parents fulfill their greatest opportunity for training other Christians.

3 EXPECTATIONS: CATCH-22 FOR EVERYONE

> "I know of no more potent killer than isolation. There is no more destructive influence on physical and mental health than the isolation of you from me, and of us from them." --Dr. Phillip Zimbardo

Expectations are like noses, we all have them and they are all different. They are difficult to live with and impossible to live without. Like the metaphorical "cultural water around us," expectations can either provide buoyancy for living or drown us.

Expectation is the act or state of expecting. It may seen unnecessary to define this word, but think for a moment about the implication. Any time we expect something, we have a mental picture of what we think should happen. If it doesn't occur, disappointment is the inevitable result.

Expectations are extremely important to the person who holds them. How many times have you heard a person remark dejectedly: "I didn't think it would be like this."

The more important the event or the relationship, the higher the expectations. Dr. Howard Hendricks of Dallas Theological Seminary believes that "the greatest reason for failure in marriage is unrealistic expectations."

We are affected all through life by the expectations we have for ourselves and by the expectations others have for us. We are in a continuing process of living up to internal and external ideals.

We rarely talk honestly and openly with each other about our expectations, but we desperately need to. When we are unable to talk about our expectations, we become involved in a game of emotional charades. We want the people closest to us to guess our expectations as we, often symbolically, act them out. When they fail to guess them, we are profoundly disappointed.

    Frustrated expectations can lead people into a vicious cycle of
disappointment and retaliation. We can see this in the breakdown
of relationships at every stage of life.
    Expectations sometimes can have a very positive effect. For
several years, a young boy was the terror of his elementary school.
No teacher dared fail him for fear of having him in her room again
next year. As he entered a new classroom one fall, the teacher met
him at the door and said:
    "Well, you must be Howard. I've heard all about you."
    "Yeah," the boy muttered. "I suppose you have."
    Then the teacher smiled and said: "But I don't believe a word of
it. I think you're going to have a great year."
    She expected something different from the boy, and she got it!

WHAT DOES SOCIETY EXPECT FROM TEENS?
IN SOME WAYS, A LOT.

Usually we expect adolescents to successfully:
Live in bodies that are undergoing dramatic physical changes.
Develop independence, maturity, and sensitivity to others.
    Begin accepting the responsibilities of adulthood even though it
will be several years before they enjoy most of its privileges.
    Negotiate an educational and social maze that exerts tremendous
pressure on some and provides others with an artificial period of
freedom and irresponsibility.

IN OTHER WAYS, SOCIETY EXPECTS VERY LITTLE FROM TEENS.

When it comes to Christian standards of honesty, morality, kindness,
and love, society has a very low expectation level.
    Because of our educational structure, we assume that most teens
will stay in school at least until age 18, and if they attend college, until age 22. We rarely expect a person to accomplish anything
significant during that time span.

WHAT DO PARENTS EXPECT FROM TEENS?

SOMETIMES, NOT ENOUGH.

We wish they were more responsible, yet we support laws that simply do not allow people to be adults until they are 18 or 21.

Some mothers expect their daughters to be <u>chaste</u>. Others encourage them to be <u>chased</u>.

SOMETIMES, TOO MUCH.

The affluent North Shore suburbs of Chicago have become known as "the suicide belt" due to the alarming incidence of teenage suicide there. A study has revealed that a major factor involved in the suicides was <u>parental expectations</u>. The parents' desire for social accomplishment by their children played a large part in creating the depression that, in some cases, led to suicide.

It takes work, risk, and faith to bring our expectations out into the open and to help our teens do the same. The process may be painful, but the potential for pain is much greater if we fail to deal truthfully with our expectations.

DISCUSSION WITH OLDER TEENS

(1) Where do you feel the most pressure, from your own expectations for yourself, or from the expectations others have for you? Why do you think this is true?

(2) What expectations do you think God has for you? Does thinking about this encourage or discourage you? Why?

(3) What has been your greatest disappointment from a parent? Have you ever discussed it together?

If not, why?

If so, what happened?

(4) As you think about your future, how can you be sure that your expectations for life are realistic and sound?

DISCUSSION WITH YOUNGER TEENS

(1) Do you think your parents usually expect you to succeed or fail in what you do?

Why do you think they feel that way?

(2) In what things do you expect to do well?

In what things do you expect to do poorly?

(3) When you go to a party, do your friends expect you to do things that your parents would expect you <u>not</u> to do?

How do you choose between the two?

(4) Have you ever talked with your parents about some of their expectations which you find hard to live up to?

If not, why?

If so, what happened?

LOOK IN THE MIRROR
FOR YOUTH WORKERS AND PARENTS

(1) Have a joint meeting of your teens and parents. Separate parents and kids, then:

Ask <u>parents</u> to list the five most important things they expect of their teens during the next year.

Ask <u>teens</u> to list the five most important things they <u>think</u> their parents expect of them during the next year.

Now, bring parents and kids together and have them share their answers with each other and compare them. You might then move to an open forum discussion of why it's so important for us to talk about our expectations and why it is often so difficult.

(2) FOR PARENTS: On a sheet of paper, list the name and age of one of your children. Then, list that child's age three years from now. For example, Mary, 14--17. (As parents, we often don't realize how old our kids will be in three years.)

Now, write the 10 most important things you expect that child to do in the next three years. You may be able to list 30, but pare it down to 10.

Next, the hard part. Share your list with that child and discuss your expectations. This gives the child an opportunity to react to your expectations in some way other than fulfilling or failing to fulfill them.

Finally, the hardest part. Ask that child to do the same for you--10 expectations for the next three years. Then discuss them.

SUMMARY

Sometimes we feel like Captain Yossarian, the anti-hero of Joseph Heller's bestselling novel, <u>Catch-22</u>. Every time Yossarian flew enough bombing missions to get sent home, they raised the number required. Catch-22.

Helping teens cope with expectations, their own and others, involves honest communication. They need to talk with youth leaders, each other, and with parents and family members. Families in our churches need to turn off the TV, turn off their prejudices, turn on their ears, and communicate with each other. If you can help that happen, you will have accomplished a great thing.

RECOMMENDED READING

<u>To Understand Each Other</u> by Paul Tournier. John Knox Press. Written for married couples but has application to every relationship of life.

4 RIGHTS: SOCIETY'S NEW BATTLEGROUND

> "Give to every other human being every right that you claim for yourself--that is my doctrine." --Thomas Paine
>
> "Men, their rights and nothing more; women, their rights and nothing less." --Susan B. Anthony

Not long ago, in Connecticut, a 16-year-old boy divorced his parents. Right now there are at least five states with "emancipation laws" that allow parents or older teenage children to "divorce" each other, thus ending all legal ties and responsibilities.

A judge who works in the family court in one of those states believes we will be seeing more and more of this in the years ahead. He says it is a result of "kids growing up too fast and parents giving up on them too soon."

When a teen today says, "I have my rights," he may be legally right and morally wrong in a way he has never been before. And if the teen isn't thinking seriously about running away from home, his mother or father may be.

One writer has called today's children's rights movement a "stepchild of the liberation struggles of the 1960s." It involves billions of federal dollars, a host of government services, and a burgeoning number of issues involving parents and the courts. It is not a simple matter.

When the Veteran's Administration found it necessary to define the word "child" recently so that benefits could be paid, it took 1,100 words across two-and-a-half columns in the Federal Register to do it.

A New York Times/CBS News Poll asked the following question: "When parents are getting divorced and having a dispute over the custody of a child, should the judge see to it that there is a lawyer who represents the child's interest, or don't you think that's necessary?"

80% of the respondents aged 18-29 said kids should have a lawyer.

Among people 65 and older, 59% said yes to a lawyer for the kids.

    In society at large, a growing number of children are involved in
legal situations in which their rights are a matter of prime concern
to them and to authorities. The legislation passed in their behalf
will also affect the teens in our lives.
    As an illustration, consider the following. (Children refers to
persons under 18 years of age.) In the United States today:

> More children are involved in marital breakups than ever before.
> As many as 100,000 children were kidnapped by their parents last
> year in custody disputes.
> More than 500,000 children are in foster care.
> 87,000 kids under 18 are in prison.
> In a recent year, there were more than 700,000 <u>reported</u> cases of
> child abuse.
> In that same year, 164,000 runaway children were taken into
> custody by police. (Glen Collins, The <u>New York Times</u>)

    Some advocates of children's rights today would send kids down
the same road of liberation as minorities and women. They say kids
should have the same rights, responsibilities, and privileges as adults.
    Others call for laws that would allow the government to assume
broader powers and to intervene in the family in cases of need.
    As Christians, we follow a Saviour who said some radical things
about rights. He spoke of taking up our cross, of finishing first by
finishing last, and of turning the other cheek. His teaching places
us and our teens at cross-currents with a society bent on having its
rights.

DISCUSSION WITH OLDER TEENS

(1) What rights do you feel you have in your home and family?

(2) What rights do your parents have in your home and family?

(3) How about the rights of your brothers and/or sisters?

(4) Which of your rights do you find consistently being violated?

(5) Have you ever discussed it with the person(s) involved?

   If not, why?

   If so, were you able to solve the problem?

(6) How does being a Christian affect what you see as your rights?

DISCUSSION WITH YOUNGER TEENS

(1) When you get your driver's license, what rights will that give
     you that you don't currently have?

(2) What responsibilities will come with those rights?

(3.) In your family, are there some rights you think you should have,
     but don't have?

     If so, what are they?

     Why don't you have them?

     Do you think you'll ever get them? Why or why not?

(4) Are there any rights you have that can never be taken from you?

     If so, what are they?

(5) As a Christian, what should you do when someone violates one of
     your rights?

LOOK IN THE MIRROR
FOR YOUTH WORKERS AND PARENTS

"I have my rights." How many jobs, marriages, romances, partnerships,
friendships, and even youth groups have been devastated by those
words?

(1) How can you find out what the teens in your life really think
     about their personal rights?

(2) Is there an area in your life where you're struggling with your
     rights and why you're not getting them?

     If so, jot down a couple of practical steps you can take in the
     next few days to begin working toward a resolution of the problem.

(3) During a joint teen/parent meeting, ask each group to list what
     they feel are their rights in the home and family. Give them a
     chance to compare answers and encourage discussion on how some
     give-and-take can occur on both sides of the issue.

(4) As a personal project, study the following passages and write
     down any thoughts they bring to mind on the subject of rights:
     a. Matthew 20:25-28

     b. John 13:1-7

     c. 1 Corinthians 9:1-23

     d. 2 Corinthians 4:5

(5) Do Christians have rights?

     What are they?

SUMMARY

Once again, we have a situation in which our culture is making a
definite statement in an area of great importance--personal rights.
Do we really know what the teens in our lives think about their own
rights? Have they expressed to us their true beliefs on which they
operate, or merely the "correct" answer which they think we want to
hear? Unless we find out, it's unlikely that we'll be able to help
them effectively cope with this area of strong cultural influence.

RECOMMENDED READING

Philippians 2 by the Apostle Paul--a chapter that points us to Jesus
Christ and how He dealt with His personal rights.

The Gospel of Mark--a fast-moving, penetrating look at the only Man
who ever had absolute power, and how He used it.

5 EDUCATION: THE ONE SIZE THAT DOESN'T FIT ALL

When you stop to think about it, kids spend a staggering amount of time in school during their teenage years. If you figure that a teen spends 8 hours a day (7 in class and 1 in activities), 180 days a year in school, the totals look like this:

1,440 hours a year in school. That's 16% of his entire life for a complete year. It also represents 25% of a teen's waking hours for an entire year. If he goes to summer school, the totals are higher.

By way of contrast, if a teen spends 4 hours a week in church activities, that's only 208 hours a year.

Junior high and high school are the two common experiences shared by almost every American teenager. Some of them love it, some hate it, and others are neutral, but everyone must cope with the experience.

LOOKING FOR THE PRESSURE POINTS

What does our culture say about education? That depends a great deal on where you are. The importance of school and its related activities may vary widely from the inner city of Philadelphia to Enid, Oklahoma, but no matter where you are, kids will be concerned with the following:

ACADEMICS If a teen expects to go to college, the pressure for grades can begin as early as junior high. Whether a student is only trying to pass or shooting for a scholarship, grades loom large as a point of evaluation. A student who does poorly academically may dismiss it with a laugh, but it usually has an effect on his sense of personal worth.

<u>ACTIVITIES</u> The farther a student goes in school, the wider the range of activities available. For some, this diversity of activities will be their salvation, rescuing them from obscurity and loneliness. For others, it may be their downfall as they overextend themselves. For kids heavily involved in church, it may represent a difficult choice, especially since more and more public schools are scheduling <u>Sunday</u> club meetings, sports practices, AND <u>ACTIVITIES</u>.

<u>TEACHERS</u> Personality clashes are in-evitable between students and teachers. If you look back at the classes you liked and disliked in school, I think you'll find them closely tied to the teachers you had. Things haven't changed and a poor relationship with a teacher can make a school year look like an eternity for your teens.

<u>SPORTS</u> Many of the high-status posi-tions in our schools are still reserved for athletes. We are a culture that re-veres football players and barely tolerates scholars and philosophers. Whether your teens are on the team, in the stands, or pretend they don't care, sports are a major part of any school scene.

<u>SOCIAL ACCEPTANCE AND POPULARITY</u>
If there is a single factor under-lying the dynamics of the modern junior high and high school, this is it. Every day is an evaluation day at school. Will he speak to me in the hall? Will she sit with me at lunch? Will I walk home by myself again today? Will they laugh when I take off my clothes in the locker room? What must I do to be a part of the "in-crowd" at school?

<u>GENERAL ATMOSPHERE</u> What kind of pres-sures are placed on a teen by his school environment? Is it expected that a good student "share" his or her completed homework assignment with others who didn't do it? If you re-fuse to cheat, will you be a social outcast? Is the general tone of the school one of cooperation with the teachers and administration, or does an "us against them" mentality exist? Who are the "cool" kids, the student leaders, and what must I do to be one of them?

In spite of all its attempts to compensate for individual differences,
modern American education is still a "one size fits all" proposition.
If you are going to help your teens cope effectively with school, you
will need to understand the dynamics of their particular educational
setting, and help them function as Christian individuals within it.
For some, it will be easy. For others, school may be the most
difficult experience of their teen years. In either case, it can
become an opportunity to discover more of their interests, talents,
gifts, and abilities.

DISCUSSION WITH OLDER TEENS

(1) What do you like best about school?
    What do you like least about it?

(2) What is the most difficult thing for you as a Christian at your
    school?

(3) Write down five things you would like to achieve or honors you
    would like to receive before you graduate from high school.
    What do you think your chances are of achieving them?
    Would you have to compromise your Christian beliefs to achieve
    them?

(4) In what ways do your parents help you in coping with school?
    In what ways don't they help?

(5) How would you rate your Christian witness at your school? Use
    a scale of 1-10 with 10 being high.
    What would it take to improve it?

DISCUSSION WITH YOUNGER TEENS

(1) Which teacher at your school has helped you the most? How?

(2) If you could change one thing about your school, what would you
    change?

(3) List all the reasons you can think of that you would like to go
    to:

    a. A public school

    b. A Christian school

(4) What aspect of school makes you feel best about yourself?
    What makes you feel worst?

    (It isn't necesary to discuss this in a group if kids will write
    their answers and think about them for a few minutes.)

(5) Ask students to complete the following sentences:

    "When it comes to _________________________ at school, I feel
    helpless."
    "If I could change one thing at my school, I would . . ."
    "When I think about living as a Christian at school, it makes
    me feel . . ."

LOOK IN THE MIRROR
FOR YOUTH WORKERS AND PARENTS

(1) How well do you know what the teens in your life are facing at school?

What can you do to become better informed about it?

(2) Was your school experience a good or bad one?   Why?

(3) Are you expecting your teens to duplicate your school experience in terms of attitude, experiences, and success?

If so, how can you overcome that tendency and help them approach their educational experiences as unique individuals?

(4) Are most of your efforts aimed at criticizing your teens' school situation or working constructively to improve it?

How can you turn this around?

SUMMARY

It is important to help teens remember that though they probably cannot choose their school, teachers, classmates, or coaches, they can choose their attitudes in every situation of life. And their attitudes can make the difference in any situation. If Jesus Christ is at the very center of their lives, then school is another place to walk with Him and another opportunity to find that He can use them in the lives of others.

RECOMMENDED READING

<u>Is There Life After High School?</u> by Ralph Keyes. Warner Books. A witty, incisive and often irreverent look at the world of the average American high school student.

6 DIVORCE AND THE CHANGING FAMILY

> "If any one factor influences the character development and emotional stability of an individual, it is the quality of the relationship he experiences as a child with both of his parents. Conversely, if there is one experience that people suffering from severe emotional illness have in common, it is the absence of a parent through death, divorce, or a time-demanding job." -- Dr. Armand M. Nicholi
>
> Harvard University Medical School

THE TREND TOWARD FAMILY FRAGMENTATION

Unless society does a dramatic turnaround, these current statistics aren't likely to change significantly in the next few years. Today's figures will still be in the ball park a decade from now.

    38% of first marriages will fail.
    90% of divorcees will remarry.
    59% of second marriages will fail.
    1 million children a year will be involved in divorce cases.
    1 of every 5 families with children will be headed by 1 parent.

Nearly half of all the children born this year will live "a considerable time" with only one of their parents before they are 18.

Children from single-parent families will continue to experience more difficulties adjusting to school and society than their counterparts from two-parent families. (based on a number of reliable studies)

Inflation and changing social values will push a growing number of women, including many mothers of young children, into the work force.

WHAT THE STATISTICS MEAN

More and more kids in your youth group will face the divorce of their parents and the experience of living in a single-parent family.

A growing number will find themselves part of a "recombined" family as two parents, both with children from former marriages, marry and merge the two families.

If your church is among the many (and I hope it is) reaching out specifically to single adults, the number of kids you meet from fragmented families will be even higher.

You will be dealing with a growing number of teens who have never experienced a stable family life and who have few Christian role models in the area of marriage and the family.

Instead of focusing on what's wrong with society and lashing out against that in your youth group meetings, you will be called on to help teens make the best of a less-than-perfect situation.

1 WHAT CAN YOU DO ?

Be Alert to Personal Needs

Many teens blame themselves for their parents' marital breakup. The following question was posed to a group of teens whose parents were divorced: "Do you think you caused your parents' divorce?" 65% of them answered yes.

In other cases, the blame is laid directly on them. One divorced mother told her daughter: "I hate you and I hate your father. Our divorce would never have happened if you hadn't been born." That girl carried the guilt of her parents' divorce until she was able to share it with a young Christian woman who helped her overcome it.

2 Understand Their Everyday World

When you talk about family relationships, you're going to have to expand your thinking. "Children obey your parents" is still a valid biblical truth but some of your teens may be wondering, "OK, which parents? My mother during the week and my father on weekends? My mother and stepfather? My father and stepmother? Whomever I'm with at the time?" Many family relationships are complicated today and you need to be ready to help kids understand them and work through the tough questions they face within their families.

3 Listen to What They Really Believe

Sandy Larsen has called attention to a dangerous flaw in much of our Christian education by noting that in church, kids tend to give us "correct answers" yet live their lives on the basis of entirely different beliefs. To effectively communicate the truth about marriage and the family to our teens, we must first find out what they _really_ believe. That takes listening, a lot of listening.

4 Stimulate Family Growth and Development

In researching a book about healthy families, Dr. Blair Justice and his wife Rita found that successful or effective families share some common traits:

- They have a positive outlook.
- They do not become overly concerned or stressed by unpleasant events.
- They are good problem-solvers.
- They possess high initiative and are resourceful. They take action rather than waiting for someone else to rescue them from a dilemma.
- They are not necessarily democratic institutions. They have agreed that the parents have the authority to act while encouraging their children to make more decisions as they mature.

The Justices noted that one of the successful families they interviewed had a runaway teenager. Another had an alcoholic father. It wasn't that they had no problems, but that they were healthy enough to do something about their problems.

DISCUSSION WITH OLDER TEENS

NOTE: You're already aware that "family, parents, and divorce" is an
emotional subject. Sometimes committed Christian teens with strong
biblical convictions can inhibit discussion if they insist on correct-
ing and refuting every non-biblical opinion given. Set your discussion ground rules to allow free expression of all opinions, and speak
to any potential problem participants privately, ahead of time, if
necessary.

(1)   Do you think you will ever get a divorce? Why or why not?

(2)   How would you rate the quality of your family life right now?
      Good, Average, Poor?   What would it take to improve it?

(3)   What do you think are the five ingredients needed by a family in
      order to be successful? (After teens list and discuss their
      ideas, you might share Dr. Blair Justice's five characteristics
      and let them compare.)

(4)   Are there any ways in which you disagree with how society views
      marriage and the family today?

(5)   How does being a Christian help a person deal with family dis-
      appointments and tragedies?

DISCUSSION WITH YOUNGER TEENS

(1) Young teens often enjoy a role-playing situation. Ask five kids
to create the following scenario:

It is 11 p.m. on a Friday night. Sitting in the living room are:

    MOM--Who works as a first-grade teacher.
    DAD--Who has been gone all week on business and just returned
        home at 8:30 that evening.
    HIGH SCHOOL SISTER--Who is 17 and grounded because of low
        grades.

Into the room walks JUNIOR HIGH BROTHER, 13, who was supposed to
be home at 10 p.m. Who says what to whom?

After a few minutes GRADE SCHOOL BROTHER, who is 8, comes in,
having been awakened by the discussion.

After the kids create the situation as they think it would
usually happen, ask them (or another group) to do it in a more
effective problem-solving way. Discuss which way is easier to
portray and why.

(2) If you could change one thing about your family, what would it
be?

Do you think you really can change it?   Why or why not?

(3) Sometime, try giving your young teens a 5- or 10-minute "gripe
session." Tell them that for the next few minutes, they may
complain about anything relating to their families. Then,
just _listen_. No comments, no corrections, just listen. At the
end, move on to something else. Later on, do some thinking and
praying about what you heard, but don't pass it on to anyone else.

(4) What is the biggest thing about which you and your parent(s)
disagree?

Do they understand your point of view?

Do you understand theirs?

(5) In what ways do you think God is like your earthly father?

In what ways is God different?

LOOK IN THE MIRROR
FOR YOUTH WORKERS AND PARENTS

(1) Armed with the knowledge of what successful families are like,
how can you help build those characteristics into the lives of
the teens with whom you work or live?

(2) How many parents of kids in your youth group do you know
personally?

What specific steps can you take to get to know more of them?

(3) Dr. Armand Nicholi, Harvard Medical School psychiatrist, says
that the only way he can find the time necessary for his family
relationships is to schedule them into his day and give them
no less priority than a medical emergency. How are you doing
in giving time to your family?

SUMMARY

"Kids are being forced to cope with a whole new world of shocks and
stresses . . . and yet they find themselves suddenly stripped of the
single best buffer against those shocks and stresses, the old-fashioned
family. Just when they need it most, the family is disappearing
before their eyes." (Sources and Resources, 8-15-81)
    If we are going to help teens cope with culture, we will have to
help them deal with the fragmented family.

RECOMMENDED READING

If I Were Starting My Family Again by John Drescher, Abingdon.
Helpful and realistic insights into being an effective Christian
parent.

"The Fractured Family" by Armand M. Nicholi. And following articles,
Christianity Today, 5-25-79, pages 10-22.

7 PEER PRESSURE: WHERE THE RUBBER MEETS THE ROAD

> "The need for acceptance in a group is the most powerful
> of the forces which mold young people's decisions."
>
> -- National Board of Junior
> Achievement Report

There are several things that we as adults need to realize about peer pressure in a teen's life:

It is a natural part of growing up. The process of becoming mature involves a progression that looks like this:

IDENTITY

Family—————⟶ Peer—————⟶ Individual

Childhood———⟶ Adolescence———⟶ Adulthood

A child gains most of his identity from his family for the first 10 or 12 years of life. Then the focus shifts to peers. Later, the individual develops a sense of who she/he is as a person, quite apart from anyone else. But instead of each stage cancelling out the one ahead of it, each builds on the previous one(s). All through life, we place importance on family, peers, and self-perception. John Donne captured the lifelong human experience in his words: "No man is an island, entire of itself."

Peer pressure, like all the other factors we are considering,
exists as an ingredient blended into the total cultural experience.
It is virtually impossible to consider it in isolation, just as it
is impossible to consider identity, the family, sexuality, or school
in isolation.

Kids react differently to peer pressure. For some, it will involve
stress, struggle, and possible abandonment of their parents' values.
Others will be hardly fazed by it.

Kids with strong, healthy self-images will cope with peer pressure
far better than those with shaky opinions of themselves. But here is
where we are often fooled, because the beautiful cheerleader, the
jock, or the National Merit Scholar may be the one whose self-image
is languishing in the lower regions.

People with a lot of answers don't help teens with peer pressure
and self-image. People who listen are the ones who help them. One
young woman who has worked professionally with high schoolers for
several years told me:

The power of peer pressure as a force during adolescence is a
changing thing. Consider these survey results indicating who and
what had the greatest impact on teenage values and behavior in:

1960	1980
1. Mother, father	1. Friends, peers
2. Teachers	2. Mother, father
3. Friends, peers	3. TV, radio, records, cinema
4. Ministers, priests, rabbis	4. Teachers
5. Youth club leaders, counselors, advisers, scoutmasters, coaches, librarians	5. Popular heroes, idols in sports, music
6. Popular heroes, idols in sports, music	6. Ministers, priests, rabbis
7. Grandparents, uncles, aunts	7. Newspapers, magazines
8. TV, records, cinema, radio	8. Advertising
9. Magazines, newspapers	9. Youth club leaders, etc.
10. Advertising	10. Grandparents, uncles, aunts

(Chart from a report prepared by Robert Johnston Co., Inc. for the
National Board of Junior Achievement.)

TAKING ADVANTAGE OF THE SITUATION

Look for the positive uses of peer pressure. It has been said that in order to best influence teens, involve them with people who demonstrate the character traits you are trying to teach.

I became interested in personally studying the Bible when a high school senior invited me, a sophomore, to a Saturday night group. He also came by and picked me up in his car. Many of the kids in that group where older than I and all of them were convinced that studying the Bible was the greatest thing since peanut butter. Their values had a profound effect on me.

We often make a point of separating older and younger teens in order to best meet their needs in a youth group situation. But there is also a case to be made for bringing them together on regular occasions, especially if your older teens have personal commitments to Christ and an interest in the young teens.

Peer pressure is no more to be feared than puberty or high school graduation. Without it, teens can never develop into responsible adults. We must recognize peer pressure as a fact of life and normal development, and begin preparing teens to cope with it in a positive way.

Develop a tradition of excellence in your youth group. Instead of youth group leadership being a job that is foisted off on just anyone, it should represent a privilege and a responsibility.

DISCUSSION WITH OLDER TEENS

(1) What do you like most about the kids you go around with?

(2) What bothers you most about the group of kids you are involved with most of the time?

(3) Who is the person in your life who has the greatest positive influence on your behavior?   Why?

(4) Who is the person in your life who has the greatest negative influence on your behavior?   Why?

(5) When it comes to the group of kids you are usually with, what does Romans 12:1-2 mean to you?

DISCUSSION WITH YOUNGER TEENS

(1) Assume that your family has just moved to a new city where you don't know anyone and no one knows you. As you think about making new friends, list several qualities you would look for in the kids you meet.

(2) Ask three teens to create a role play situation in which a mother and father are talking to their teenage son or daughter about his/her friends of whom they don't approve.

Be sure to have the "parents" name the kids they don't approve of (make up imaginary names) and tell why they don't like them. The "teen" in this role play can react in any manner he/she pleases.

After the role play, discuss the statements and reactions of both parents and teen, then perhaps have your players reenact the scene in a way that would promote more understanding.

(3) Why do you think parents get involved in their children's choice of friends?

Should parents stay out of it?

How could parents be more helpful when it comes to your choice of friends?

(4) What does Proverbs 13:20 mean to you in choosing friends?

LOOK IN THE MIRROR
FOR YOUTH WORKERS AND PARENTS

(1) In what ways do you as an adult still face peer pressure?

(2) In what ways does your youth group exert positive peer pressure on its members?

In what ways is the pressure negative?

What steps can you take to emphasize the positive?

(3) As you consider the teens in your life, what three steps can you take to help them cope more effectively with peer pressure in their individual lives?

SUMMARY

Peer pressure cannot be avoided, but it can be used as a positive force and a growing experience in the life of every teen. When Christ is a valued friend, what He wants assumes its proper place in our lives.

8 MASS MEDIA MAZE: LOOKING, LISTENING, LEARNING

There is perhaps no greater area of controversy between teens and adults than the one concerning music, movies, magazines, books, and television. Much of it stems from the fact that teens are growing in their independence and they desire to make their own choices. At the same time, parents still feel responsible for the input their children receive.

The issue is complicated by the permissiveness of our time, and the ineffectiveness of most attempts to label and regulate who sees and hears what. A PG-rated film could be an innocuous story with a little gratuitous violence added to avoid the "G" rating, the kiss of death in the industry. On the other hand, a PG film could have its protagonists swearing profusely, making bets on who can lose her virginity first, or taking vengeance on insensitive classmates by dismembering them through the use of psycho-kinetic powers.

In some ways, our culture's mass media could be personified as a man who has installed a wave-making machine in a sewage treatment pond and opened it as a "surfing beach." The incredible thing is

that adults and teens are flocking there in droves, paying a high admission price to get in, then calling back over the fence, "Come on in. The water's fine!"

TALK AND LISTEN

<u>When you have an objection to something, discuss it.</u> Sounds simple, but it isn't. Discussing involves listening and we are usually so intent on getting our point across that we could care less what the other person thinks or how he/she feels about it.

DEAL WITH FEELINGS

<u>Realize that you are dealing with emotion, not intellect.</u> The teen years are a time of strong feelings. You may well be able to assess the good and bad aspects of a film or book from an intellectual perspective, but a young person, first and foremost, <u>feels</u> a certain way about it. When you combine a teen's desire for independence, peer pressure, and the attractiveness of the media item in question, you have all the ingredients of a pubescent Mt. St. Helens.

EXPLAIN YOURSELF:

<u>Try to explain what you object to, even if it sounds silly.</u> My young daughters have a book titled, <u>The Bears of the Air</u>, by Arnold Lobel. After a few readings, I decided it was very subtly against some things I believe as a Christian. It's a cute story about four little bears who live in a cave with their old grandfather. Grandfather has a book titled, <u>Things a Good Bear Should Do.</u> But the little bears never can do any of those things, even though they try. So they do their own things, and in the end they get Grandfather out of a jam by being their own little persons. From that time on, he uses his book just to sit on while he watches his four super-smart grandsons.

One night I tried to explain to my daughters why I didn't like that book. I felt silly, but I think it was the right thing to do. We still read lots of books together, but not that one.

PROVIDE GREAT ALTERNATIVES

Offer teens some outstanding alternatives to what they can't have. Dr. Jack Mitchell, a great old saint and teacher at Multnomah School of the Bible, used to say: "Don't knock what I've got unless you can offer me something better." That's exactly where we are with our teens.

The trouble with our alternatives is that they often don't match the mass media offerings we object to. If you object to most movies, what are you offering instead? No rock and roll at your house? Is there another choice besides "easy listening" or a musical vacuum?

AVOID THE DOUBLE STANDARD

If they can't have it, then can you? If you don't want your teens to see certain films, don't go yourself and then use them as illustrations in your talks. If the kids can't watch a certain movie on TV, should you watch it yourself? Hypocrisy has long been the chant of teens against parents and other adults. The only way to silence it is to avoid it.

STRUGGLE TOGETHER

Try watching/listening/reading selected things together and struggle with them as a team. One of the biggest difficulties in today's society is that teens consume vast amounts of mass media input _alone_ and they must process and cope with it by themselves. In some cases, I believe we need to choose certain TV shows, songs, movies, or books and experience them together. Then we need to talk together about what they say and mean. Encourage parents of teens in your church to become fellow travelers with their teens and not just media traffic directors.

I have a friend who drops into his high school daughter's room from time to time as she listens to her favorite Top 40 radio station. They'll listen to a couple of songs, then talk about them. They discuss the words, what they say, and what the song is all about. She moans and groans about her dad's "record talks," but she isn't having to cope with her culture alone. Besides, her dad is getting a real education through it.

DISCUSSION WITH OLDER TEENS

(1) Where do you and your parents most often disagree regarding mass media? (Movies, music, TV, or other things?)

(2) What is the usual outcome of your disagreement?

(3) What don't you understand about your parents' point of view?

What _do_ you understand?

What don't they understand about your point of view?

(4) What could you do to improve communication and lessen conflict in this area?

(5) How old is old enough when it comes to certain movies?

How mature does someone have to be to see an X-rated film?

DISCUSSION WITH YOUNGER TEENS

(1) List three movies you would like to see, but can't see.

Why can't you see them?

In what ways does that bother you?

(2) List three movies you could see, but have decided not to see.

Why did you decide not to see them?

(3) Do you think that certain TV shows, songs, or movies are harmful to you in some way? If so, which ones and why?

(4) Have you ever seen a movie, read a magazine, or heard a story that you wish you hadn't been exposed to? Why?

LOOK IN THE MIRROR
FOR YOUTH WORKERS AND PARENTS

(1) Are there any limits which you impose on your own mass media consumption?

What are they and why do you have them?

(2) Is there a big difference between the mass media you experienced as a teen and what is offered today?

If so, try to express that difference in a few sentences.

Have you been able to communicate your feelings on this to the teens in your life?

(3) Are there any concepts in this chapter with which you disagree?

What are they and why don't you buy them?

What alternatives do you suggest?

SUMMARY

The day will soon come when the teens in our lives will go where they like and see what they want without our guidance. We can either use these years to build a wall around them or help them build Christian convictions that will guide them through life.

9 LOVE IN THE AFTERNOON: WANDERING IN A SEXUAL WILDERNESS

> "People who are in love don't follow society's standards, only their own. And if they both think it's right for them--beautiful." -- A 16-year-old girl
>
> "Being a virgin is of no importance in marriage. Marriage is only a commitment to love and be loved by one other person." -- A 16-year-old boy

Teenagers have had to contend with sex and sexuality for a long time. But it seems today, that the rules are far different from what they've ever been before. As one man described the situation: "We used to turn our young people loose in the wilderness, give them a map and say, 'Here, find your way through all this back to civilization.' Now we turn them loose and tell them, 'There is no map anymore.'"

Once again, statistics give us a point of reference for what's happening in society:

One out of every five teenagers has sex by age 13 or 14.
Half of all high school seniors are sexually active.
One out of every 10 girls ages 15 to 19, becomes pregnant.
Nearly half of all teen marriages break up within five years;
Marriages resulting from pregnancy have an 80% divorce rate.
Venereal disease is now an epidemic, and only 10% of its victims
    have any adequate understanding of the disease.
6% of the nation is homosexual.
More than half of all black babies in the United States now are
    born out of wedlock and the trend is increasing sharply among
    whites, especially teenagers.
Abortion is being increasingly used by women of all ages as a
    means of birth control.

WHAT TEENS FACE TODAY

1
Mass media exposure that glorifies and promotes sex.

2
Advertising built on a basic premise-- sex sells.

3
More frank and open presentation of sex as a natural activity of life, subject only to a person's individual feelings on the issue.

4
Promotion of homosexuality and lesbianism as viable, alternative lifestyle choices.

5
Society's expectation that teens will postpone marriage in order to complete their education.

6
Christian expectation that teens will remain celibate during that time. For many, this means that for some 10-15 years, they must cope with an intense sexual drive without yielding to the temptation of having intercourse outside of marriage.

7
A society and in many cases, a church that has all but abandoned biblical standards of sexuality and morality.

8
A peer group that is sexually active on a much wider scale and at a much younger age than ever before.

9
A breakdown in the traditional family, and in communication with parents at a time when it is desperately needed.

10
A society that offers few adult role models who are effectively coping with their own sexuality and able to help a teenager cope with his or her own from a Christian perspective.

WHAT NEEDS TO BE DONE

➡ Promote open, honest communication between parents and teens on the subject of sexuality.

➡ Encourage teens to read and discuss books that present a positive, biblical approach to coping with sexuality.

➡ Lead teens into a study of the Bible and its teaching on sexuality.

➡ Guide teens into discovering ways to express and celebrate their sexuality beside erotic activities.

➡ Discover what the teens in your life really think about sex. Ask questions, listen, let them ask questions that concern them.

➡ Create an environment that will promote serious consideration of sexuality for each teen in your life, despite the diversity of their ages, experiences, and levels of maturity.

DISCUSSION WITH OLDER TEENS

(Often, many teens may be reluctant to discuss these questions in a serious vein. One approach to overcoming this is to distribute a list of the following questions and have your teens write only the number of the question and their answers on 3" x 5" cards. Use a separate card for each question. Collect the cards, organize them according to question number and then read and discuss the answers. You can be selective about which answers you read, thus eliminating the written wisecrack and the non-serious answer. You can also quell the tendency to guess who wrote the answer to each question.)

(1) What is the dumbest thing anyone ever said to you about sex?

(2) What is the most intelligent thing anyone ever said to you about sex?

(3) When it comes to what your church teaches about sex, what do you disagree with most?

(4) As you observe your friends at school, what do you think is the biggest mistake they are making in the area of sex?

(5) Complete the following: "The greatest problem Christian teen-agers face today in regard to sex is . . . "
(Remember, only you can determine the appropriateness of this type of discussion with the teens in your youth group. You may feel these questions are better suited to one-on-one counseling or to groups of all guys/gals. The goal here is honest dialogue and mostly listening and learning on your part.)

DISCUSSION WITH YOUNGER TEENS

Again, 3" x 5" cards and anonymous answers may help you overcome the awkwardness of this age. Also, remember that there is a vast difference between 12- and 14-year-olds when it comes to a serious interest in sex.

(1) Why do you think the Bible says that people should be married before they have sex together?

(2) Do you agree with what your parents think about sex?

Why or why not?

(3) If you had a question about sex, whom would you ask?   Why?

(4) Does being a Christian make any difference in your life when it comes to sex?   If so, what is it?

(5) Why would God make people able to have intercourse and produce babies when they are 12 or 13 and expect them to wait long after that to get married and have sex?

LOOK IN THE MIRROR
FOR YOUTH WORKERS AND PARENTS

(1) How effectively would you say you are coping with your own
sexuality as an adult?

       Well   Fairly well   Poorly

What do you need to do to become more effective in this area
yourself?

(2) What influences in your life tend to warp your view of sexuality?

(3) What influences help you to keep a proper perspective on it?

(4) Where did you learn the most about sex as a child/teen?

Is that the source from which you want the teens in your life to
get their information?

What can you do to see that their knowledge comes from helpful,
caring Christian sources?

SUMMARY

Sex is one of God's gifts to each of us. By knowing Him and His
purposes for our lives, we will discover the real meaning of our
sexuality. Culture makes its statement about sexuality in a hundred
ways each day. We too must make a statement to our teens that is
biblical, compassionate, and real.

RECOMMENDED READING

Eros Defiled by John White, Inter-Varsity Press. An outstanding
biblical approach to our modern sexual wilderness.

10 ARTIFICIAL ADULTHOOD: THE TRAPPINGS OF INDEPENDENCE

> "The real test for Christian character is not creed or conduct . . . but motive. God is more concerned about your motives than anything else in your life."--Richard Halverson, Manhood with Meaning

Remember the "adolescent iceberg" in chapter 1? It reminded us that much of what's happening in a teen's life is below the surface. This chapter deals with what's happening at the iceberg's tip--above the water for all the world to see. These are the things many teens do as part of trying to establish their identities as adults.

Our consideration of drugs, alcohol, and the like comes purposely late in this Power Pak. For too many people, helping teens cope with culture begins and ends with these practices. We can't ignore what's happening at the iceberg's tip, but we should not focus on it to the exclusion of everything else.

WHAT DO BIG FOLKS DO?

If you'll spend a few moments reflecting on some of the advertising images present today, several patterns of exclusively adult behavior emerge. Adults are people who:

End every working day by having a beer in a homey spot surrounded by lots of attractive, happy friends.

Use tobacco.

Fall in love, enjoy sex together, possibly even get married.

Drive cars, travel, use credit cards, and spend money on whatever they please.

Surround themselves with material things that bring them a great deal of happiness.

These are the images we see every day on TV, in films, in news-papers, magazines, and on billboards. Real-life role models often reinforce these images. A conclusion begins to form in the minds of kids that says: "I want to be grown-up and free so I can . . . "

Occasionally, culture does us an unexpected favor. Today, for exam-ple:

There are fewer kids using hard drugs than in the 1960s.

The number of kids smoking has dropped over the past few years.

The worldwide emphasis on health, nutrition, and physical fitness has had an impact on many teens.

On the other hand:

More kids are drinking alcohol and at an earlier age than ever be-fore.

Marijuana is a significant prob-lem and only now are the real medi-cal facts regarding its effects being discovered.

Many of the things with which kids experiment today are poten-tially more destructive in a shorter period of time.

Once again, the challenge is to help teens work <u>through</u> these issues. Of course we want them to avoid as many mistakes as they can, but they need more than pronouncements from above. One of our greatest tasks is helping them decide what constitutes genuine adult-hood.

WHAT CHARACTERIZES THE TRULY MATURE PERSON?

1   A respect for the law and for others. It balances privileges with responsibilities.

2   An ability to make a contribution and help others in my present situation. An adult is someone who should be part of the solution, not part of the problem.

3   Problem-solving skills that enable a person to squarely face difficulties and disappointments, and move on in spite of them.

4   Physical, financial, emotional, and spiritual independence that enable a person to live on his own, apart from his/her parents.

5   Self-discipline that enables a person to maintain a consistent pattern of behavior even under difficult circumstances.

6   Personal convictions and goals that free a person from the opinions and standards of others, yet do not violate the rights of others.

Artificial adulthood counterfeits these characteristics, usually with activities or practices that promise an easy route to the achievement or appearance of maturity. A teenager may <u>feel</u> independent by smoking a cigarette in public, taking a drink, or becoming involved sexually with another person, but it is only a feeling. True maturity involves much more and takes much longer.

DISCUSSION WITH OLDER TEENS

(1) When confronted with a temptation to use alcohol, tobacco, or drugs, which question most affects your decision?

Is it legal for me?

What if I get caught?

Will I please God by doing this?

Will this bring me pleasure?

(2) Are there any other questions that enter into your consideration?

If so, what are they?

(3) What do you think are the characteristics of a real adult, a truly mature person?

(4) Read James 1:2-4 in the Phillips translation. What is the process that God puts us through to help us develop true maturity?

(5) What are some things we may be attracted to that seem to offer a shortcut to adulthood?

In what ways do these things produce a kind of "artificial adulthood"?

DISCUSSION WITH YOUNGER TEENS

(1) Do you know any adults who haven't really grown up?

If so, what are some of the things about them that bother you?

How do you think you can avoid becoming like that?

(2) When an adult brings up the subject of smoking, drinking, or drugs, do you listen or turn off? Why?

(3) People of all ages do a lot of things to try to "escape" their problems instead of facing them. Why do you think we do that?

What other choices are there besides escape?

(4) What are some _good_ ways you have found to demonstrate your independence and _your_ increasing maturity?

(5) Why do you think God has commanded us _not_ to do certain things?

What are we going to miss by obeying Him?

LOOK IN THE MIRROR
FOR YOUTH WORKERS AND PARENTS

(1) Do you often, perhaps knowingly, encourage the teens in your life to embrace an "artificial adulthood" by the stories you tell of your own adolescent experiences?

(2) Take a survey with your teens in which you ask the following:

    a. List all the things to which you think your parents expect you to say no.

    b. List all the things to which you think your parents expect you to say yes.

    c. If it were strictly up to you, what things would you add and subtract from each list?

(3) In what ways do you still face the temptation to embrace an "artificial adulthood" even though you may be well on the other side of 21?

SUMMARY

One problem with any sin is that once we become involved in it, we are more likely to figure out why what we are doing is right, rather than why what we are doing is wrong. We tend to develop a theology that allows us to be comfortable in our chosen lifestyle.

The final line for us and our teens is how we cope with culture based on our response to the lordship of Jesus Christ in our lives. Will we follow society's shortcuts to maturity or base our actions on personal conviction and faith?

RECOMMENDED READING

<u>Be Yourself and God's</u> and <u>Manhood with Meaning</u> both by Richard Halverson. Zondervan. Penetrating essays on what it means to be mature as a person and as a Christian.

<u>Extraordinary Living for Ordinary Men</u> by Sam Shoemaker. Zondervan. Capturing the excitement of a life of adventuresome faith.

11 SERVICE: WHAT ALL WANT TO GET AND FEW WANT TO GIVE

Recently, I asked a youth director if it is possible for a Christian teenager today to live a committed, holy life among his peers and still be liked and respected by them. His answer:

Of all the kids in my church, I know only one who is doing that, and it's only because she lives as a servant to others. She's the one who drives the spikes into the starting blocks at the track meet while everyone else is doing her personal warmups. After a school party or dance, she's the one who stays around to clean up. She's willing to take the jobs behind the scenes that no one else wants, let other people have the credit and be content just to serve. She's the only kid I've ever had in a youth group like that, and the people she goes to school with know that she's a Christian because she serves.

We live in a culture that is great at demanding service, but knows little of how to give it. Service for the sake of serving is almost unheard of these days. Some people are willing to serve because of the financial rewards, others because their employer insists on it, but we as Christians are called on to approach life with the attitude of the Apostle Paul who wrote:

"For we do not preach ourselves, but Jesus Christ as Lord, and ourselves as your servants for Jesus' sake." (2 Cor. 4:5, NIV)

ASSESSING THE CULTURAL CLIMATE

How many people do you know who say "servant" when asked what their career ambitions are?

Where are the attractive adult role models whose lives will challenge teens to serve others?

When was the last time you encountered a Christian leader who personified Jesus' words: "Whoever wants to become great among you must be your servant, and whoever wants to be first must be your slave." (Matt. 20:26-27, NIV)

Why do we who claim to follow Jesus Christ demonstrate so little of His servant attitude in our daily lives?

Who is going to teach the teenagers in your life to serve if you don't do it?

A few years ago, I attended a party at the headquarters of a Christian organization in our city. In order to accommodate the people, we rearranged the furniture in the room where we met. Following the party, a man began rearranging the furniture as it was before our gathering. Others of us joined in helping him as he straightened the room, picked up cups and engaged in general cleanup.

I was impressed because the man leading the cleanup was the president of the organization whose facilities we were using. But instead of standing around expecting others to do the dirty work, he joined in and led the way. As I have observed his life over the years, I have come to realize that he truly is a servant of others. That evening wasn't unusual, but is the norm in his life. Even in his role as an executive, he works to serve others.

Our culture defines greatness in terms of fame, wealth, and achievement. Jesus defined greatness in terms of service. If we are to help our teens make an impact on their world for Jesus Christ, we must help them confront our Lord's teaching about service.

DISCUSSION WITH OLDER TEENS

(1) In what restaurant did you receive the worst service (not food) you have ever had?

Why was it so bad?

What about the best service you ever received? Where did you receive it and what made it great?

(2) What do you think it means to be a servant of Jesus Christ?

In how we treat Christ Himself?

In how we treat our families?

In how we treat people at school and at work?

(3) Why is it so difficult to be a genuine servant of others?

(4) In what situation of your life did you learn the most about serving others?

What did you learn?

DISCUSSION WITH YOUNGER TEENS

Bring a basin of water, a bar of soap, and a couple of towels to your youth group meeting. Have one or two kids go around and wash the feet of some of the other kids. (It may get a bit rowdy, but it will be worth it.) Then discuss the following:

a. Is there a story about something like this anywhere in the Bible?

b. What do you remember of the story without looking it up?

c. Read John 13:1-17 and discuss why Jesus got up to wash His disciples' feet.

d. Who should have done it?

e. What do you think their feet were like after the disciples had walked around the streets of Jerusalem all day in sandals? (Do some research on the situation so you can fill in the cultural details to make the scene live for your teens.)

f. What do you think is the modern equivalent of washing people's feet?

g. Since washing other's feet isn't a part of our culture today, how can we carry out Jesus' command to serve others?

LOOK IN THE MIRROR
FOR YOUTH WORKERS AND PARENTS

(1) List one or two ways in which you can be a servant of the people with whom you work and live each day.

(2) In a society that enjoys being served, how do we develop the
attitude of wanting to serve others and looking for opportuni-
ties to do it?

(3) In what situation of your everyday life are you likely to expect others to serve you?

Is there any way in which your attitude needs to be reconsid-
ered in light of Jesus' example?

SUMMARY

Servanthood isn't something we're likely to learn from our culture.
Society says get while Christ says give. True greatness for our
teens and the door to making an impact on their world may swing on
the hinges of service to others.

RECOMMENDED READING

Borden of Yale by Mrs. Howard Taylor. Moody Press. A classic
biography of a young man whose life was defined by the phrase "no
reserve, no retreat, no regrets."

His Thoughts Said . . . His Father Said by Amy Carmichael. Christian Literature Crusade. Timeless insights into God's solution to
our human confusion about giving and getting.

12 RESCUE THE PERISHING: OR LET THEM LEARN TO SWIM?

A continuing dilemma of adults involved with teens is the issue of when to step in and how to help with their problems.

RESCUING DEFINED

By resuing, I mean taking action in a situation to relieve the pressure on a teen. It may involve removing the teen from a particular place or set of circumstances. Or it may consist of shifting the blame for the pressure from the teen to another source. In either case, rescuing is getting a teen _out of_, rather than helping him or her _go through_ a pressure situation.

- If a teen is having a horrible time getting along with the kids at his junior high school, should the parents move in, take him out of that school and transfer him to another?
- If a student athlete is in academic trouble, should his parents set up an enforced study time, ground him from all social activities and pull him through? Or should they let him make the choice of failing and losing his athletic eligibility?

● A 7th-grader's science teacher is
very vocal about his belief in evolu-
tion and his humanistic philosophy of
life. Should a parent go to the school
and have the student placed in the
class of another science teacher who
happens to be a Christian?

● If a young person in charge of ar-
rangements for a church youth function
doesn't get the job done, should the
youth director step in and do it or let
the young person fail?

● To what degree should a parent
regulate a teen's music, reading mate-
rials and television viewing?

● What lessons should we let teens
learn on their own and which do we
spare them by moving into a situation
that seems to be beyond their control?

Obviously, I can't tell you what to do in the situations I have
just listed. You must determine your own course of action based on
the situation as you know it and your personal convictions. I would,
however, make some observations about our tendencies in this area:

1

We tend to get into a "rescuing posture" too quickly and too
often.

As adults, we often overreact to pressure on a teen, especially
when that pressure is causing pain and we can do something to relieve it. Instead of thinking how we can get involved with teens and
help them work through an issue, we tend to begin thinking how we can
get them out of the situation.

2

School is as likely as anything to provoke a Christian parent
or youth director into rescuing.

We all know the importance of school in the lives of teens. In
today's society, there often exists an "us VS them" mentality between
Christians and the public schools. If we think a teacher or situation is unfair to a teen in our lives, we are often too quick to step
in with our brand of adult authority and influence.

3

If we choose to rescue by regulation (telling teens what they
can and can't do), we can regulate only the part of a teen's life
that we can see.

Regulation may be a valid aspect of any adult/teen relationship,
but it should be part of a larger process of developing internal,
independent thought and action. Regulation by itself leads only to
an enforced behavior in the presence of the enforcer.

4

Failure is seldom fatal.

The older we grow, the more we realize the truth of this in our
own lives, but fail to accept it in the lives of our teens. In order
to succeed, you must also have the right to fail.

DANGERS OF RESCUING

We teach teens that the best way to deal with a problem is to get away from it. Instead of helping them work through it, we teach them to look for a way out of it.

They never learn to deal with unreasonable people. Junior high principal Don Wallace says: "I'm convinced that if parents don't teach their kids to deal with unreasonable people before they go to college, they may never learn it." Strong words. Something to think about.

THE SCRIPTURES

What does the Bible say about this particular problem? If I don't know, then I need to study it personally before speaking to a teen about the issue.

In Galatians 6:2 we read the command to "carry each other's burdens, and in this way you will fulfill the law of Christ." It paints the picture of one person getting under a burden being carried by another, and helping him carry it. Rescuing simply tries to remove the burden.

TIME

James 1:2-4 tells us to "let the process go on until that endurance is fully developed" (Phillips). This is difficult to do in our own lives and doubly difficult when the pressure is hurting a teen we love. Our resource is God's wisdom (James 1:5) and His promised guidance for the person who asks in faith, ready to obey.

As adults, we tend to overreact when our teens encounter pressure. We must be willing to invest the time necessary to help teens work through instead of using rescuing as a quicker and easier alternative.

OBJECTIVES

What are the results this pressure should produce in the lives of our teens? Do we want them to learn to love an unlovable person; to deal with unreasonable people; to accept injustice and make the best of a situation if it can't be changed?

Unless we think through the lessons to be learned in each situation, we will be ineffective in helping our teens learn them.

ARE THERE TIMES WHEN I SHOULD RESCUE?

One of our goals as adults is to give our teens tools they can use in solving their problems. There may be situations in which they have employed those tools, have tried their best to cope with things, and it appears that the pressure may be too much for them. Yes, there is a time when an adult must move in and say, "That's enough" and take steps to change the situation. Only you can determine when that is.

DISCUSSION WITH OLDER TEENS

(1) Do your parents tend to "rescue" you from difficult situations or help you work through them?

In what ways do you wish their approach was different?

(2) How often do you turn to the Bible to find help in trying to cope with a particular problem?

How effective do you find the Bible in helping you?

(3) Look up the following passages and write down one thought from each about working through difficult situations:

James 1:2-5

1 Peter 2:18-21

Hebrews 12:7-13

(4) If you found a problem too much to cope with on your own, to whom would you turn for help? Why?

DISCUSSION WITH YOUNGER TEENS

(1) Read Matthew 5:44. Is this a realistic way to deal with someone
     who hates you?   Why or why not?

(2) Are there times when you find it difficult to ask your parents
     for help with a problem?   If so, when?

(3) If you had a teacher at school who was grading you unfairly and
     not doing a good job of teaching the class, how would you handle
     that problem?

     If you told your parent(s) about it, what do you think they
     would do?

(4) Have you ever prayed with one of your parents about a particular
     problem?

     How would you feel about doing that?   Why?

LOOK IN THE MIRROR
FOR YOUTH WORKERS AND PARENTS

(1) Do you see pressure as a positive or negative factor in life?

(2) In what ways might you be drawn into "rescuing" the teens in
     your life?

(3) Do you have a tendency to overreact when your teens face pres-
     sure and pain?

     How can you transform that desire to rescue into a positive,
     helping involvement with your teens in working through the prob-
     lem?

(4) As a youth director, in what ways might you be unconsciously
     involved in "rescuing"?

SUMMARY

A friend of mine tells the story of his aunt who had polio when she was a child. All through her life, she had a hand that shook constantly. She walked with a limp because she could never put her heel to the ground. But the reason she went through life as a cripple was that her mother refused to let her go through the pain of therapy as a child. She couldn't bear to see her endure pressure and pain in order to grow.

Can we afford to "rescue" our teenagers from the very experiences they need to become mature Christian adults?

RECOMMENDED READING

<u>Too Big to Spank</u> by Jay Kesler. Regal Books. Practical advice from a national youth leader on parenting teens.

CONCLUSION

Not long ago, I attended a conference for people involved in ministry with single adults. One well-attended seminar was titled: "Helping God's Dream Come True for Your Single Adults." The idea behind the title was that this seminar would equip us to offer significant help and encouragement to the single adults with whom we were working.

The seminar leader began by discussing self-esteem. After 10 minutes, it was obvious that those of us in the group were focused not on our single adult friends back home, but on ourselves. The man leading the seminar was talking about our needs, our hopes, dreams, successes, and failures. He was dealing with life as we lived it and we all knew that we could use his insights and help.

I trust that a little of this has happened as you've studied this Power Pak. During my research for this writing, the single most repeated theme from youth workers, psychologists, pastors, parents, teachers, and counselors was: "Unless we as Christian adults get our act together and begin to cope with culture ourselves, we won't be of much help to the kids." One reason today's teens have so much trouble coping with culture is we adults who are supposed to be helping them are not coping with it well ourselves.

The best thing we can do for the teens in our lives is to become effective persons as we deal with the world around us. May God help us to follow Him through life in such a way that we will be able to mark His path for others.